Rapping about
What animals eat

Bobbie Kalman

Crabtree Publishing Company

www.crabtreebooks.com

Rapping about series

Created by Bobbie Kalman

For my cousin Benedek Varga,
a carnivore, herbivore, folivore, florivore, frugivore, granivore,
nectarivore—a very hungry omnivore,
who loved my cooking and asked for more

**Author and
Editor-in-Chief**
Bobbie Kalman

Editors
Kathy Middleton
Crystal Sikkens

Photo research
Bobbie Kalman

Design
Bobbie Kalman
Katherine Berti
Samantha Crabtree
(logo and front cover)

Print and production coordinator
Katherine Berti

Prepress technician
Katherine Berti

Illustrations
Barbara Bedell: pages 12
Katherine Berti: page 17 (termite)
Bonna Rouse: page 8
Margaret Amy Salter: page 9

Photographs
BigStockPhoto: page 12
(bottom right)
iStockphoto: page 21
Photos.com: page 10 (center)
Other images by Shutterstock

Library and Archives Canada Cataloguing in Publication

Kalman, Bobbie
    Rapping about what animals eat / Bobbie Kalman.

(Rapping about--)
Includes index.
Issued also in electronic formats.
ISBN 978-0-7787-2798-9 (bound).--ISBN 978-0-7787-2805-4 (pbk.)

    1. Animals--Food--Juvenile literature. I. Title. II. Series:
Rapping about--

QL756.5.K347 2012   j591.5'3   C2011-907715-9

Library of Congress Cataloging-in-Publication Data

Kalman, Bobbie.
Rapping about what animals eat / Bobbie Kalman.
p. cm. -- (Rapping about--)
Includes index.
ISBN 978-0-7787-2798-9 (reinforced library binding : alk. paper) --
ISBN 978-0-7787-2805-4 (pbk. : alk. paper) -- ISBN 978-1-4271-7913-5
(electronic PDF) -- ISBN 978-1-4271-8028-5 (electronic HTML)
1. Animals--Food--Juvenile literature. I. Title. II. Title: What animals eat.

QL756.5.K357 2012
591--dc23

2011046211

Crabtree Publishing Company
www.crabtreebooks.com   1-800-387-7650

Printed in Canada/022012/AV20120110

Published in Canada
Crabtree Publishing
616 Welland Ave.
St. Catharines, Ontario
L2M 5V6

Published in the United States
Crabtree Publishing
PMB 59051
350 Fifth Avenue, 59th Floor
New York, New York 10118

Published in the United Kingdom
Crabtree Publishing
Maritime House
Basin Road North, Hove
BN41 1WR

Published in Australia
Crabtree Publishing
3 Charles Street
Coburg North
VIC 3058

Contents

Living things

Animals are **living things**.

Living things are alive.

Food gives animals **energy**
to grow, move, and survive.

Some animals eat mainly plants.

They are called **herbivores**.

Other animals eat mainly meat.

They are called **carnivores**.

*Rabbits are herbivores
that eat grasses and flowers.
They feed on these plants
for hours and hours.*

Omnivores are animals that eat both plants and meat. Omnivores are not fussy about the kinds of foods they eat.

This fox is an animal that prefers to eat meat, but it cannot always find animals to eat. When it is hungry, it eats plants, too. For this omnivore, any food will do.

Grass eaters

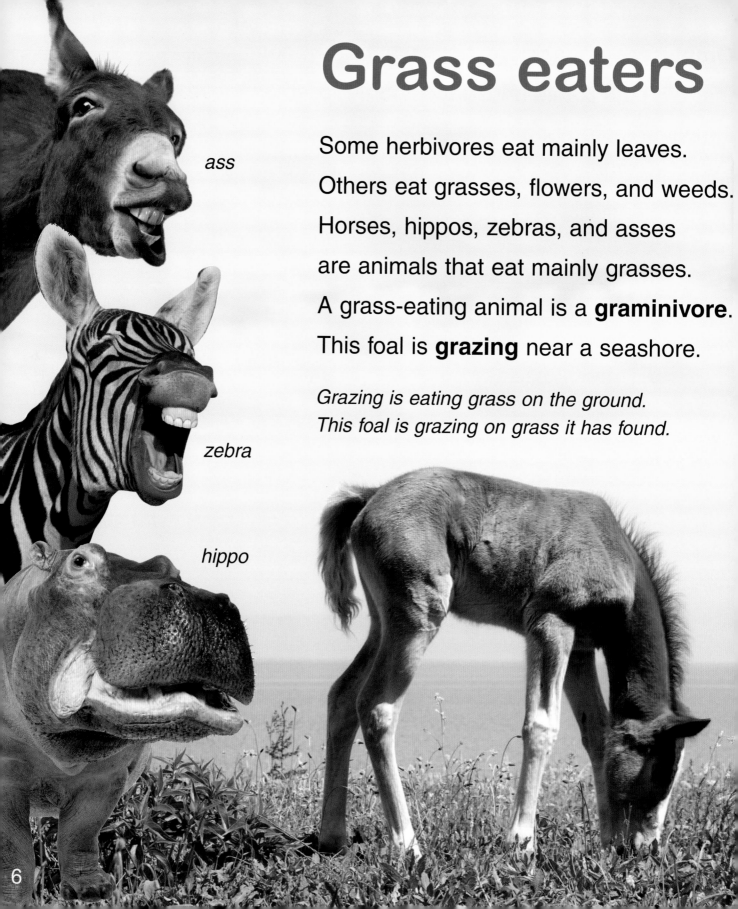

ass

zebra

hippo

Some herbivores eat mainly leaves.
Others eat grasses, flowers, and weeds.
Horses, hippos, zebras, and asses
are animals that eat mainly grasses.
A grass-eating animal is a **graminivore**.
This foal is **grazing** near a seashore.

*Grazing is eating grass on the ground.
This foal is grazing on grass it has found.*

Grasses also grow at the bottom of seas.

Manatees and sea turtles feed on these.

*This ocean grazer is a manatee. It belongs to the **sea cow** family.*

This green sea turtle is a herbivore, as well as an undersea graminivore.

Leaf eaters

Many herbivores **browse**, or eat leaves.
Folivores are leaf-eaters like these.
Some browsers are also graminivores,
and both kinds of eaters are herbivores.

Giraffes can reach the tops of trees. Their long necks help them reach the leaves with ease.

Moose and elephants
are big animals
that need a lot to eat.
They eat leaves, grass,
flowers, and fruit,
but they don't eat
any meat!

This caterpillar folivore eats mainly leaves.
It finds food on many plants and trees.
After it turns into a butterfly,
it finds another kind of food to try.
It no longer needs to chew its food.
Instead, it drinks **nectar** through a tube.

9

Feeding on flowers

Animals that eat flowers are **florivores**.
Those that eat nectar are **nectarivores**.
Some eat **pollen**. They are **palynivores**.
These parts of plants that grow outdoors
are all foods eaten by herbivores.

A groundhog is a herbivore.
When it eats flowers, it is a florivore.

Which insects drink sweet nectar?
Which one is a pollen collector?

Inside flowers,
liquid nectar is found,
plus a powder called pollen,
which is yellow, white, or brown.
It is a part of flowers,
that honeybees carry around.

Honeybees eat nectar
and pollen to stay alive.
They put pollen in their baskets,
to take back to their **hive**.

pollen

pollen
basket

Fruits and nuts

Frugivores eat mainly fruit.

The ones shown here are very cute.

Some mice, lemurs, bats, and apes,

like pears, guavas, berries, and grapes.

Some lemurs and bats are frugivores.
Fruit is their favorite meal.
They eat every part of the fruit—
even the seeds and the peel.

dormouse

lemur

bat

Granivores eat nuts and seeds. They find these foods in flowers and trees. Chipmunks stuff them in their stretchy cheeks and then bury them for the cold winter weeks.

nuts

acorns

Squirrels collect acorns and nuts and hide them in the fall. Sometimes they hide the nuts so well, they cannot find them all.

seeds

pine cones with seeds

Predators

Carnivores eat mainly meat.

Predators hunt the animals they eat.

The animals they hunt are called **prey**

How could these prey get away?

This spider has hunted a frog in a tree.
Will the frog be strong enough to break free?

A rat makes a meal
for a big bird like this.
With such a long beak,
the bird cannot miss.

A leopard drags an antelope
high up a tree to eat.
Dragging a big animal so high
must be quite a feat!

Insectivores

Insect eaters are called **insectivores**.

They are predators as well as carnivores.

Butterflies, beetles, grasshoppers, and more are insects eaten by insectivores.

Most bats catch insects while they fly.
Bats can hear insects in the dark, night sky.

butterfly

bee

Bee eaters eat bees, wasps, and ants.
They catch these insects on many plants.

fly

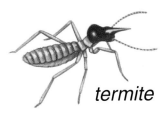
termite

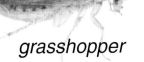
grasshopper

ant

This frog sees a fly nearby that it would like to eat. It sticks out its long, sticky tongue to grab this tasty treat.

skunk

Some insectivores eat the grubs

that live under the ground.

Armadillos, skunks, and voles

know just where grubs can be found.

armadillo

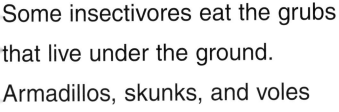

grub

beetle

17

Cleaning up

Eating and being eaten are parts of **food chains**.

What predators don't eat, a **scavenger** gains.

When the predators leave, the scavengers fe

They often can find all the food they need

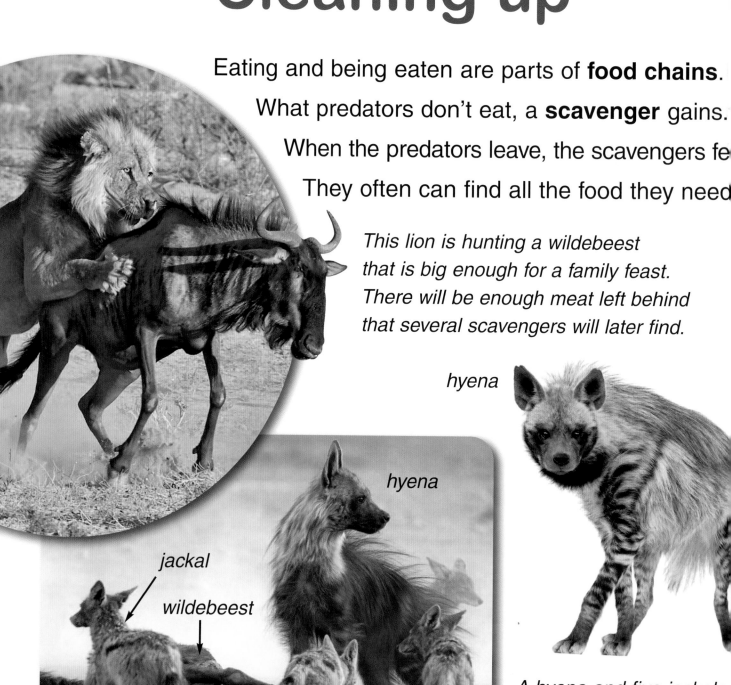

*This lion is hunting a wildebeest
that is big enough for a family feast.
There will be enough meat left behind
that several scavengers will later find.*

hyena

hyena

jackal

wildebeest

*A hyena and five jackals
found the lion's prey.
There is plenty of dinner
for all of them today!*

millipede

Detritivores eat the wastes they find—
the parts that scavengers leave behind.
Worms, beetles, maggots, and flies
clean up the earth after something dies.

fly

snails

cockroach

dung beetles

earthworm

maggots

19

Omnivores eat it all!

Omnivores eat any foods they find—
meat, plants, and fruit of every kind.
Omnivores have a good chance to survive.
Their eating habits keep them alive.
Raccoons, bears, foxes, and skunks
are omnivores, and so are chipmunks!

skunk

fox

raccoons

chipmunk

bear

People omnivores

Did you know people are omnivores, too? We use our omnivore teeth to chew. Our front teeth are sharp for tearing meat. Our **molars** can grind the other foods we eat. What is your favorite kind of food treat?

When you eat meat, you are a carnivore.
If you eat only veggies, you are a herbivore.
If you eat both, you are an omnivore.
If you eat foods grown close to home,
*you are a **locavore**.*

Match them up!

Some of the words in this book are hard,
but learning them is really fun.
Match the words to the "eaters" shown,
and you'll learn every one!

1. A plant eater is a herbivore.
2. An eater of other animals is
   a carnivore.
3. An eater of plants and animals
   is an omnivore.
4. A leaf eater is a folivore.
5. A flower eater is a florivore.
6. A grass eater is a graminivore.
7. A seed and nut eater is a granivore.
8. An insect eater is an insectivore.
9. A fruit eater is a frugivore.
10. A pollen eater is a palynivore.
11. A nectar eater is a nectarivore.
12. A cleaner of dead things is
    a detritivore.
13. Someone who eats foods grown
    near their home is a locavore.

(A) *bee*

(B) *bee eaters*

(C) *fly*

(D) *butterfly*

(E) *zebra*

F
child with vegetables grown in her garden

G *lemur*

H *giraffe*

I *lion*

J *squirrel*

K *rabbit*

L *raccoons*

23

Glossary

Note: Some boldfaced words are defined where they appear in the book.

carnivore A meat eater

detritivore An animal that eats the leftover waste of dead things

energy The strength needed to grow, change, move, and do physical and mental activity

florivore A flower eater

folivore A leaf eater

food chain The pattern of eating and being eaten

frugivore A fruit eater

graminivore A grass eater

granivore A seed and nut eater

herbivore A plant eater

hive The home of honeybees

insectivore An insect eater

living thing A plant, animal, or person that needs sunlight, air, water, and food

locavore A person who eats foods grown close to home

molar A flat back tooth that is used for grinding food

nectarivore A nectar eater

omnivore A living thing that eats plants and animals

palynivore A pollen eater

scavenger An animal that feeds on the leftovers of prey hunted by other animals

sea cow An animal such as a manatee, or dugong that lives in water

Index